GOTHS

Dan Vice

Crombie Jardine
PUBLISHING LIMITED

13 Nonsuch Walk, Cheam, Surrey, SM2 7LG
www.crombiejardine.com

This edition was first published by Crombie Jardine
Publishing Limited in 2005

ISBN 1-905102-24-0

Written by Charlotte Hathaway
Illustrations by Helen West
Designed by www.mrstiffy.co.uk
Printed and bound in the United Kingdom by
William Clowes, Beccles, Suffolk

With special thanks to
Rachel Wright, who is
DEFINITELY NOT
a Goth.

CONTENTS

CHAPTER ONE

THE DARK AND MYSTERIOUS WORLD OF GOTHS

I   By Means of Introduction

In a world obsessed with social classification, it is impossible to walk the streets of our nation's cities without being confronted by stereotypes at every turn. Although Chavs may be the most common, they have a sworn enemy: the subculture known nationwide as 'Goth'. If Chavs are represented by the disillusioned working classes, so Goths are the disillusioned middle classes. This group shall now be subjected to vice-like scrutiny as I attempt to define the indefinable.

To be a Goth is to be unique, creative and misunderstood. However, in order to be considered truly 'gothic', it is necessary to conform to certain Goth norms. Your gothness is then measured by your peers with a 'gothier-than-thou' approach, facing ridicule if you are falling short.

ii Some Popular Goth Myths and Stereotypes

✠ *They're all Satanists*

✠ *They're all suicidal*

✠ *They're always miserable*

✠ *They think they're vampires*

✠ *They never smile (because this would crack their make-up and stop them from looking cool)*

✠ *They have to wear black all the time*

✠ *They are all Marilyn Manson fans*

✠ They enjoy taking black and white photos

✠ Like cats, they can only see in shades of grey. This is a popular explanation for an unimaginative choice of colour (or rather tone) combinations. In reality, their eyesight is usually so poor that they must navigate using enormous trousers to detect movements. The downside to this, of course, is that given a good gust of wind, Goths have been known to blow away. On

*the flip side of this, the subclass
of this subculture, Minigoths, have
been known to make excellent kites.*

Though these stereotypes are
largely myth, there are of course
still some (mostly wannabes and
Minigoths) who will adhere to
them religiously. Contrary to
popular belief, most Goths do in
fact have a sense of humour and
don't take themselves as seriously
as people like to think. However

there are exceptions to every rule
and I shall hide in safety behind
my pseudonym in case the hive
has been stirred and angered
by this light-hearted guide.

iii A Brief History

Historically, the term 'Goth' comes from the ancient Germanic tribe of the same name, which divided into the Ostrogoths and the Visigoths. In 268 C.E. the Visigoths invaded the Roman Empire and took over the Balkan Peninsula, controlling much of Europe in the Middle Ages. A style of art and architecture soon developed, but was seen by the intellectuals of the Renaissance as crude, to be held in contempt. The gothic was associated with the uncivilised, the barbarian. However, although 'gothic' became a derogatory term, people were captivated and preoccupied with the notions of good versus evil, death, and purity versus decadence. As time progressed, a wealth of literature, art, and architecture burst forth.

The Romantic movement of the late 18th and 19th centuries had its roots in Gothicism; leaders in

the field are well known writers
such as Lord Byron, Mary Shelley,
and William Blake. The Victorians
repressed the sensual nature of the
Gothic; but the morbid flourished.

Modern Goth culture raised its ugly
head in the early '80s, beginning
with a style of music, a component
of the punk-rock scene (with
offshoots such as Souxie and the
Banshees). This developed into
its own genre as the former died

away. It has now spawned an entire subculture with its own uniform, philosophy, and unwritten rules.

Internationally speaking, terminology for this species to be found abroad is as follows:

✠ *France: coneille, gothique, goth, corbeau*

✠ *Germany: grufti, gotik*

✠ *Holland: gothiek, gootje*

✣ *Japan: gosurori, cosplayers, Yamamba (a witch from Japanese folk tales)*

✣ *Mexico: darks, gotico, darketo, darky*

✣ *Spain: siniestro, gótico*

✣ *Sweden: got, svartrock*

✣ *USA: Goth.*

CHAPTER TWO

A GUIDE TO GOTH SPOTTING

I CATEGORIES OF GOTH

✠ *Minigoths / Baby Bats*

A very common type of Goth. These tend to be the young teenagers who gather in huge groups around shopping centres, and are often not considered to be 'true' Goths. Some may progress in later years to the more advanced stages of gothness and adopt one of the categories that follow. However, for many, it is just a phase. A Baby Bat is also a newcomer to the Goth scene,

and who may not be completely
savvy with the culture yet.

✠ Tradgoths / Romantic Goths
These tend to veer towards
the classical gothic, with
Edwardian and Victorian
style clothing, and a great
interest in gothic literature.

✠ Vampire Goths
These find vampires cool and
sexy (vampire is of course

spelt 'vampyre'). They actually look a bit like vampires.

✠ Fetish Goths
Like leather, PVC and chains a lot. Are likely to partake in BDSM (bondage, discipline and sado-masochism).

✠ Pagan Goths
Into Wicca, the occult and Celtic religions. Tend to resemble the more witchy side of the gothic.

✠ Perky Goths

Dress in a more modern fashion,
like computers, and also fetish.

✠ Raver Goths

Wear those very large flares with
fluorescent things all over them.
Are very easy to see in the dark.

✠ Goth Geeks

Not the same as ordinary geeks.
Honest. They wear modern
clothes and can be found in
'alternative' pubs playing

Magic (a role-playing card
game). They often display their
gothness via internet webrings.

✠ **Cybergoths**
They like EBM (Electronic
Body Music) and hang
around techno clubs.

✠ **Ren Faire Goths**
Like the Renaissance Faire and
role-playing games. Easily spotted
by their medieval style clothing.

✠ Mopey Goths

The gentler type of Goth.
Their style of clothing is
usually romantic or modern.

✠ Slut Goths

Unpopular with most of the
Goth scene, these tend to wear
very tiny skirts and crowd
surf in the mosh pit.

✠ Metalheads

Usually wear black military
combats with pockets on each

side for holding CDs, a t-shirt
depicting some favourite
band, and heavy boots. They
are most likely to be found in
a pub with a pint in one
hand, and head banging.

This list is by no means
exhaustive. Of course Goths
are all individuals and cannot
be categorised. Can they?

ii   How to Identify a Goth

In case you are unsure of
what a Goth looks like, when
out Goth spotting for the first
time, here are a few hints.

✢ *The age of a Goths is irrelevant;*
they are timeless. However the
young ones do attract scorn
from the elders along with
accusations of being wannabes.

✢ *They are pale, miserable-looking,*
dramatic and overly-romantic,

and congregate in large groups
(especially Minigoths). They all
seek to look pale and interesting.

✠ They like cool, damp, dark
places, and prefer not to be out
in daylight lest they dissolve.
They do not like open spaces,
preferring to blend in with a
suitable wall or alleyway. The
comfort of the group helps them
to avoid the agoraphobia that no
doubt ensues when left alone. And
when on the move, they tend to

stick to the edges of the street, away from the road, scuttling quickly from shelter to shelter.

✠ The easiest way to tell if what you have spotted is in fact a Goth is to look at their hair and clothing. Black is popular in both these fields, and also in make-up. However other colours may also be used, for example deep purple, blood red, and other shades of the night. The faces are on the whole pale, and many favour to cover

their true looks with countless
piercings. This is believed to
help protect their delicate skin
from the harshness of daylight.

✠ The style of clothes is usually
classed as 'alternative' by the
politically correct. With the
female of the species, corsets,
black lace, flowing dresses and
heavy boots are popular. As
well as mini-skirts, chains and
fishnet tights. Striped stockings
are also seen. The males are

often indistinguishable from the females. They are recognisable because (usually) they are not wearing a corset, and often wear trousers. Dramatic coats are common, and top hats are coming back into fashion. They tend to look like rather classy (but dead) opera-goers, or men covered in so much metal you suspect they may have had an accident in a car-crushing compound. Velvet is always in fashion, crushed or otherwise, and lots of it.

✠ Hair is generally long and black or Schwartzkopf Cosmic Blue. Styles are unisex, and Goths take great pride in their hair. Undercuts or wool dreads are popular, highlighted with strange colours. Make-up is pale, with lips painted red (or black for the more teenage-angst driven Minigoths). Eye make-up is big, with squiggly things drawn around the eyes with eyeliner.

However this is risky as other Goths can tell when it looks bad and it is liable to smudge in damp air. Goths have a tendency to cry eyeliner, not tears.

✠ Goths like to wear plenty of silver jewellery, especially with occult and religious symbols, although they don't usually know what they mean. Spiky collars stop them from scratching their fleas.

iii Goth Hotspots

Goths are very much a city
phenomenon; in rural areas
they are scarce or non-existent.
(Cities such as Newcastle, London,
Manchester and Bristol are
infested.) Theories behind this
include the already mentioned
fear of open spaces, and the need
for a large group. In a rural area
it would be hard to find fellow
Goths, and so those unfortunate
enough to live in the country tend
to migrate to the cities at the first

opportunity. You do get a few on
council estates and in poor urban
areas, but then they run the risk of
persecution from the Chav types.
Glasgow is a prime example of Chav
(or Ned) versus Goth warfare.

Camden has been described as a
Goth Heaven (or Hell if that is
what they prefer), and you will be
able to see them there in droves.
This would make a good Goth-
spotting day-trip. Whitby is a

must: as well as being the spot where Count Dracula landed when he came to Britain, it is also home to the Goth Festival twice a year – in August and at Halloween.

Most big cities will have a Goth pub or two: for example, The Hobgoblin and Hatchets in Bath; The Full Moon, The Eclipse, and The Bierkeller in Bristol; Scruffy Murphy's and The Colmore Bar in Birmingham; The Auld Hoose

and Jekyll & Hyde in Edinburgh;
and The Devonshire Arms and the
Intrepid Fox in London. Every
Saturday, The Slimelight in London
is probably the most popular of
Britain's Goth clubs. In Bath on
Monday nights, many Goths can
be spotted at The Playground
(although it is so dark you can
hardly see them for the black).
Their unique way of dancing must
be noted — a kind of rock and sway
from side to side, occasionally

moving the arms. Listen out for
the loud bangs of their heavy boots
as they approach. The boots are
loosely done up so that they hit
the ground before the feet do.

Other good places to look for
Goths include your local cemetery
(of course), bookshops, specialist
Goth shops (for example, Shrinking
Violet is a leader in its field),
libraries (if lacking the money
to buy books, a Goth will go

to any lengths to brush up on
the essential literature), on the
internet. Shopping centres and
central areas of towns are good for
Gothlets, particularly the covered
market in Bristol, Eldon Square
in Newcastle, and outside City
Hall in Belfast. Music festivals
are also good because there you
will find all types of everything.

IV Goth-Spotting Tips for the Amateur

✝ At night their dark clothes make Goths invisible, and often all that can been seen is a group of disembodied floating heads, the light reflecting off their many piercings. It is advised that you carry a torch while on an expedition. However, as this does run the risk of frightening them off, a supper of carrots may do the trick — thus enabling the Goth spotter to see in the dark and avoid artificial light.

✠ In broad daylight, you are more likely to see Minigoths, and sighting a full-grown Goth is rare and an occasion to be treasured.

✠ The older ones tend to be friendly and mostly harmless; however the Gothlets are as obnoxious as any other youth stereotype. Beware if thinking of approaching the collective.

✠ A good bear trap covered in
  dead roses wouldn't go amiss
  for the enthusiast.

✠ A favoured technique by the
  less experienced Goth spotter is
  to dress up as one and brave a
  gathering. This is not advisable as
  they can smell a fake a mile off.
  Unless you are really convincing
  and know what you are doing,
  this tactic should be avoided.

✠ *Full moon is a good time*
to embark on a Goth-
spotting expedition.

✠ *Goths can often be found*
in the parts of town you
haven't been to before. This
is why they gather there.

✠ *Don't look them in the eyes.*
They'll know what you're up
to and won't be too forthcoming.
Similarly, it's best to keep

notepads and cameras to
a minimum. Restraining
orders are not fun.

✠ And lastly, enjoy yourself! A
clever person once said 'the
Goth is entitled to the same
kind of treatment as any normal
human being; however witty
satire can't hurt anybody.'

CHAPTER THREE

GOTH PHILOSOPHY

İ   An Outsider's Perspective

Goths are seen as disenchanted
middle-class kids who don't really
have anything to rebel against and
are depressed by the futility of
their lives. So they demonstrate
their individuality by dressing
and acting like every other Goth
in the country (of course there is
a certain criteria to be adhered
to before you are considered a
'true' Goth). They feel rejected by
society, and sit around depressed
and miserable, but are also smug

because they are part of something esoteric that lesser mortals cannot understand. They make a big scene about wanting to be left alone in their misery; however, they do want to be seen. It is all about the effect.

They were more than likely bullied at school.

This is of course an unfair over-generalisation adopted by the ignorant who are not Goths.

ii   RULES OF THE GOTH CLUB

✠ You do not talk about
  the Goth club.

✠ The first sign of being a Goth
  is denying it — 'I am not a Goth,
  I am an Individual'.

✠ Anybody who admits to being a
  Goth is not a true Goth but just a
  wannabe and therefore to be scorned.

✠ People younger than you are
  not true Goths — they are
  Minigoths, Quasigoths, wannabes
  etc. They are clearly copying you,

even if they have never met you.

✟ The more obscure something is, the cooler it is. If more than two people have heard of a band you cannot admit to liking it.

✟ Only the ignorant are happy.

iii The Aim of 'Gothism'

In theory being a Goth is all about beauty and acceptance – finding beauty in things that others find disgusting or taboo, like death. However 'Goth' means something different to each follower. Goths they tend to be pacifist and apathetic, although there are examples, such as in Glasgow, where they have taken on militant form to combat the Chavs (or Neds, as they are known in Scotland). Chavs are the ultimate enemy – a Metalhead

Goth once said to me: 'Chavs are the bane of society. They should all be neutered so that they do not pollute our glorious gene pool.'

Goths reject the mainstream, seeing the emptiness of the popular culture and fashion victims. Initially they sought a higher plain of existence, found refuge in poetry and appreciated art. However, this is more of a Tradgoth philosophy as many would prefer to destroy pop altogether.

Dressing as a Goth has become a form of rebellion against the parents and society in general. You wear your persecution as a badge – you're not a Goth until you've been abused in some way by lesser mortals.

IV Religion

Many Goths would consider themselves atheist, or adhere to personal philosophies such as 'live for metal, die for metal', or 'honour, pride, respect'.

Others may belong to any of the world's major faiths, but more frequent among Goths are religions such as:

✝ *Wicca*

✠ *Druidism*

✠ *Satanism (these tend to be Marilyn Manson fans)*

✠ *Shamanism*

✠ *Other neo-pagan traditions.*

Much of the gothic can be drawn from Medieval Christian belief, and this is a source of inspiration for album titles, gothic names, etc. However these themes are often given a darker and ironic twist.

CHAPTER FOUR

HOW TO BECOME A GOTH: TEN SIMPLE STEPS

1   CHOOSE YOUR GOTH NAME

For this you need to use a little creativity, because it is not cool to have the same name as somebody else. Remember: your name must reflect your inner Goth self, so choose wisely, and think pretentious. Popular are:

✝ *Names from films and television, such as Drusilla, Reagan or Mortitia*

✝ *Names from literature*

and mythology, such as
Lestat, Ophelia, Lillith,
Mina, or Vladimir

✠ Misspelled 'ordinary' names,
where the 'i' is replaced by
a 'y', and everything is spelt
in the most archaic fashion
possible. Letters such as 'x'
and 'z' are also common

✠ Animal names such as
Raven or Viper

✠ Emotions and sensations

such as Darkness, Sickness, Agony, or Fury

✠ Biblical or demonic names, such as Beelzebub and Balthazar

✠ Scary sounding names such as Punisher, Black Vomit, Darknorth, or Noctrus

✠ Also, the longer names like Raven The Dark Rose, Morbid Angel, Beautiful Nightmare, Bloody Rose, Deadly Whisper, and Father Of All Lies.

As Goths tend not to spawn young
(this would spoil the image and
would not look cool), very few
Goth names are actually found on
birth certificates. Do not worry
that your own birth certificate
declares you to be Cecil Cuthbert
Carruthers – you will soon find
your inner Blackness Of Sweet Pain.

II Pick a Category

You will, of course, need to look
deep inside your gothic self for the
answer to this step. However, you
may just wish to pick the group you
think looks coolest. Unless you are
truly daring, it is not wise at this
stage to create your own category,
so one from an approved list is
advised. Remember: you are trying
to be a Goth, not an individual. If
you wanted to be an individual,
you wouldn't use this guide.

iii Update your Music Collection

This is the easy part. Although it always helps to be able to name at least one obscure band that is not mentioned on this list:

✠ *The Cure*

✠ *Souxie and the Banshees*

✠ *Sisters of Mercy*

✠ *The Birthday Party*

✠ *Alien Sex Fiend*

✠ *NIN*

✠ *Ramstein*

✠ *Lacuna Coil*

✠ *Nightwish*

✠ *Bauhaus*

✠ *The Crüxshadows*

✠ *Iron Maiden*

✠ *Inkubus Sukkubus*

✠ *Immortal*

✠ *Dark Funeral.*

Favoured by Minigoths
and Quasigoths:

✠ *Evanescence*

✚ *HIM*

✚ *The Rasmus.*

Many Cybergoths enthuse about rhythmic noise, typified by *Converter* and early *Noisex*; and EBM, such as *Front Line Assembly* and *Velvet Acid Christ*.

Tradgoths are into comedy metal, such as *Cradle of Filth*.

If you have picked the more unusual category of Goth to affiliate to, make sure you research their preferred range of Goth music.

Remember, if it is filled with death, despair, bleeding, and destruction, then it is GOOD. With most Goth music it is impossible to pick out lyrics in the general noise of anguished shouting. Simply corrupting a favourite Bob Dylan album may be equally effective.

IV Brush up on the Appropriate Literature (knowing your Rice from your de Sade)

Many Goths simply appreciate a good old Sci-fi or fantasy; however the established gothic literature is an important aspect of the 'tradition', so you should know about the following:

✢ *Anne Rice*

✢ *Bram Stoker's **Dracula***

✢ *The Countess Bathory*

✢ *Mary Shelley's **Frankenstein***

✠ ST Coleridge's **Christabel**

✠ Anne Radcliffe

✠ Gregory Matthew Lewis's **The Monk**

✠ Horace Walpole's
   The Castle of Otranto

✠ William Beckford

✠ The Marquis de Sade

✠ Edgar Allan Poe

✠ Dante's **Inferno.**

V Essential Films

As well as music and literature, you must also know your films. Here is a list of examples you may wish to look into:

✠ *Anything by Tim Burton, for example* **Batman** *and* **The Nightmare Before Christmas**

✠ *Anything with vampires in it (***Interview with a Vampire**, **The Fearless Vampire Killers**, *old series of* **Buffy** *etc.)*

✠ *Rocky Horror Picture Show*

✠ *The Crow (many aspiring Goths base their whole images around Eric Draven)*

✠ *Zombie movies generally (**Dawn of the Dead, The Evil Dead**, etc.)*

✠ *The Addams Family*

✠ *Films that are over 30 years old and in black and white are always good*

✠ Mel Brook's *Young Frankenstein*

✠ *Nightmare on Elm Street*

✠ *Edward Scissorhands*

✠ Most of the horror genre
(*Friday the 13th* and
Halloween – anything
starring Michael Myers).

VI Dress the Part

A subscription to *Gothic Beauty* magazine may be helpful in this area.

Here is a list of popular labels:

✠ *Raven (though can be quite pricey)*

✠ *Laughing Vampire*

✠ *Omen*

✠ *Dark Star by Jordash*

✠ *Cyberdog*

✠ *Deviant Clothing*

✠ *Scary Miss Mary*

✠ *Ruby Gloom*

✠ *Emily the Strange*

✠ *Swirling Dervish.*

Make-up is generally as described
in the Goth-spotting guide. 'True'
Goths claim to make their own
clothes, recalling the days when
you couldn't just go to Topshop and

buy a ready-ripped t-shirt done
up with safety pins. However Goth
shops these days provide a wealth
of ideas for the inexperienced. Find
yourself a good corset.... Go on!

VII The Art of Lurking

This is really a very simple art
to master. What you need to
remember is that shadows are
your friends. You should try to
lurk in a demure but theatrical
manner, glowering enigmatically
from your corner – this all adds
to the mysterious persona that
you are attempting to create.

If you are still a potential Gothlet,
you will want to find a group to
loiter rebelliously with. This is

best done in daylight as you are
not yet allowed out after 9pm.

It is easy to make people
suspicious and wary of you and,
if in doubt, adopt a vampiric
pose and hope for the best!

VIII   Master the Tongue / Goth Lingo

Speech is on the whole very pretentious and much of the time archaic. A good greeting is 'hail!' or sometimes even, 'infernal hail!' Others include an indiscriminate use of 'thee' and 'thy'.

Other language tends to be consistent with local dialect, including phrases such as 'You'll never believe what this townie wanker shouted at me on the street the other day,' followed by

a description of the oh-so-witty
reply they claim to have given,
but probably thought up as they
were scuttling away at top speed.

The language of a Goth is geared towards seeming intelligent and otherworldly. If you are a bit limited in the vocabulary department, it may help to read some of the previously recommended literature in order to pick up some new expressions. Remember, the more verbose and pretentious, the better.

IX Social Acceptability

Goths are just like any other
social clique, and credentials are
important. Who you know and how
you came to be part of the group
count towards your Goth points.

To gain points you must be able to
spot the popular among the crowd
and become friendly with them.
As you are just starting out, this
may take some time, but with a
little patience you may eventually
impress. The collective is generally

very suspicious of outsiders, so this will be the hardest nut to crack (metaphorically speaking).

Things that will impress are the number of piercings and scary tattoos that you have, as well as your knowledge of obscure bands, and the other topics previous mentioned. Tales of woe and personal suffering will also allow you to score highly.

X Points to Remember

✠ Anne Rice is a historian
   as well as a novelist

✠ No-one has suffered as much
   as you, or as stylishly

✠ People who mock you are just
   threatened by your awesome
   intellect and individuality

✠ Nobody could ever understand
   you fully, no matter how
   hard they tried

✠ Being a Goth is all about
   the image. You must look cool,
   but tragic, at all times

✠ By following this guide you
   admit to being a Goth and
   are therefore a wannabe.

CHAPTER FIVE

THE MATING RITUAL

İ   On the Pull

The most challenging part of picking a mate is working out whether the pretty creature dancing alluringly in the badly lit club is male or female.

In Gothworld, levels of androgyny tend to be high, and it is important not to seem to care about gender. Bisexuality is generally seen as cool (many Goths claim to be 'omni sexual'), however many men would prefer not to have to partake in

orgies / threesomes with other
men. The females are the more
genuinely bisexual, or at least
the more willing to go through
with their claims, if only to turn
on male Goth acquaintances.

A Goth may look for a variety
of different things in a mate:

✠ *the amount of metal they are able to carry on their person imbedded in their flesh*

✠ *daring hairstyles*

✠ *how close they look to death (evident through their paleness and languid appearance)*

✠ *alcohol-related attractions*

✠ *whether or not they would be willing to carry out alternative sexual acts.*

II Courtship

This will involve vomit-inducing poetry and dead flowers for many types of Goth, especially Tradgoths. There is a website which will deliver dead roses in a coffin-shaped box to your loved one for a very reasonable price.

Fetish Goths partake in rituals involving metal spikes and unpleasantness with unnatural orifices. The Goth scene has close links with the fetish scene and

BDSM. Many pretentious Goths,
to sound cool, will say that they
like pain and biting each other as a
form of foreplay, and the vampiric
connotations that go with it that
are oh-so-sexy. However, it's all
lies. Most Goths may be able to
put up with a slight nibbling,
but extreme BDSM will leave
them wailing for their mothers.

To score high Goth points and
attract the desired mate, it is

important to have things that other Goths don't have, like limited editions of JTHM (*Johnny The Homicidal Maniac*) and rare clothes. As genuinely attractive Goths are a rarity, material possessions to give you status are important. Goths are really just as shallow as us mere mortals when you get down to it.

iii Couples

While it is said that a Goth
will shag anything, you do see
the occasional couple. In most
circles you will get 'it' couples,
and these will comprise the most
female-looking looking male,
and the bitchiest actual female.
Everybody will want to be their
friends in order to gain social
acceptability. Those who are
striving to be true 'individuals'
will not manage this without
the approval of the in-crowd.

CHAPTER SIX

HOW TO INSULT A GOTH

This is sometimes difficult to
do, as Goths repel all assaults
by continuing to insist upon
their individuality and looking
down on you for not being
as individual as they are.

Of course you may never want
to insult a Goth. However,
should you feel the need, here
are a few ways of doing it:

✠ *Insult a band that they may like*

✠ Ask them what bands they like, and then declare that you have been to all of their concerts and they're not that great

✠ Tell them that Robert Smith from The Cure is a has-been, and was never worth listening to in the first place

✠ Ask them questions about being suicidal, worshipping Satan, and any of the other popular myths already listed

✠ Play loud Britney Spears and
Beyoncé music and request that
they dance to it – for added effect
sing along loudly and out of tune

✠ Call them a wannabe Goth as
there can be no greater insult.
If you call them a Goth directly
they'll just say that it shows how
little you know about subcultures.

The End

If you have enjoyed reading this book, please visit our website to see what else we have published.

www.crombiejardine.com

If you have any comments
or suggestions for other
Little Books, please email us:
goths@crombiejardine.com.

All Crombie Jardine titles are available from High Street bookshops, Amazon or Bookpost (P.O. Box 29, Douglas, Isle of Man, IM99 1BQ. Tel: 01624 677237, Fax: 01624 670923, Email: bookshop@enterprise.net. Postage and packing free within the UK).